10 9 8 7 6 5 4 3 2 1

Copyright © 2024 David Luckman

ISBN: 978-1-5271-1137-0

Published by Christian Focus Publications,
Geanies House, Fearn, Tain, Ross-shire, IV20 1TW, U.K.
www.christianfocus.com

Illustrations by Silvana Di Marcello
Design by Pete Barnsley (CreativeHoot.com)

Printed by Imprint Press, India

All words in bold are included in the glossary at the end of this book.

THIS BOOK BELONGS TO:

_____

CONTENTS

ACTS

Jesus said goodbye to his disciples and went back into heaven. In Jerusalem, his followers waited for the promised gift of the Holy Spirit. When the Holy Spirit came at Pentecost, the apostle Peter told everyone the good news about Jesus. Many people put their trust in Jesus and were baptised. They formed a new community – a **church** – filled with people who loved and followed Jesus. The Jewish leaders did not like the apostles telling people the good news about Jesus and tried to silence them. But the apostles kept on speaking about Jesus. They performed many signs and miracles too. More people believed in Jesus and the church got bigger.

Then violent persecution broke out against the church in Jerusalem. All the believers, except the apostles, fled to the surrounding areas of Judea and Samaria. They spoke about Jesus as they travelled, and many believed. A religious Jew called Saul threatened the church and hunted the followers of Jesus. He wanted to kill them and stop the good news about Jesus from spreading. On his way to Damascus, however, Saul met Jesus and was changed. Saul, the persecutor of Christians, became Paul the apostle of Christ. His mission was to bring the good news about Jesus to the Gentiles (non-Jews) throughout the Roman Empire.

And so the story continues…

ONLY BY GRACE
Acts 15:1-21

Some men came down from Judea to Antioch. They began teaching the **disciples** of Jesus that 'no one can be saved unless they are **circumcised** according to the Law of Moses.' Paul and Barnabas disagreed strongly and argued with them. The discussions were heated. Afterwards, Paul and Barnabas along with some other disciples, were chosen to go to Jerusalem. They were instructed to go to the **apostles** and elders about this issue. Having been sent on their way by the church, they travelled through Phoenicia and Samaria. They met with the followers of Jesus in these places and told them the wonderful news that many Gentiles believed the gospel and were saved. This news brought great joy to the

believers there. They continued on their journey. When they arrived in Jerusalem, they were made very welcome by the church, the apostles, and elders. They told them of all the amazing things that the Lord had done with them.

However, there were some Jewish believers who belonged to the party of the Pharisees. They spoke up, saying, 'it is essential that the Gentile believers be circumcised and made to obey the Law of Moses.'

The apostles and the elders came together to talk about the issue. They discussed it for a long time. Then Peter stood up and said, 'Fellow believers, you know that from the beginning, God decided that the Gentiles should hear the good news from me and believe. And as a **sign** of his acceptance, God gave them the Holy Spirit, in the same way that he gave the Holy Spirit to us. There was no difference between us in God's sight, because he also cleansed their hearts by faith. So, why do you test God in this way? Why are you placing a heavy burden on the disciples in a way that neither our ancestors nor we have been able to carry? We believe that the **grace** of the Lord Jesus will not only save us, but it will also save them!'

Those who had gathered together went quiet. Then they listened to Paul and Barnabas speak of what God had done through them among the Gentiles, using signs and wonders. When they had finished talking, James spoke to the assembly. 'Fellow believers, please listen to me. Simon Peter has told us how God went to the Gentiles, and from them, he made a people for himself. The words of the **prophets** agree with this. The Lord says in his Word, "After this I will return and rebuild the house of David, I will repair its broken walls and restore its ruins so that the rest of humanity may seek the Lord, even the Gentiles who bear my name." Amos 9:11-12.

'So, I think we should not trouble the Gentile believers with circumcision. Rather we should write to them and tell them to stay away from idolatry, from sexual immorality, from what has been strangled, and from blood. For a long time the Law of Moses has been read in the **synagogues** each **Sabbath**, and his words are preached everywhere.'

WHAT'S THE POINT:

The Judeans wanted new Gentile believers to be circumcised according to the Law of Moses. But Paul saw this as adding something extra to the gospel of salvation. They had heated arguments with the Judeans about it. In Jerusalem, the apostles turned to the Scriptures, and the way forward became clear. We are saved only by the grace of the Lord Jesus. No one can do anything to save themselves from sin, or to help save themselves from sin. It is a free gift from God. God's salvation changes how we live.

LOOK BACK:

Read Amos 9:11-12

Those called by God's name are in a saving relationship with God. It has always been God's intention to include the Gentiles in the people of God!

CHECK THIS OUT:

Read Acts 15:19-21 and James 1:22

James shows in simple detail what the *holy* life looks like. In his letter, James is clear that true faith in Jesus *always* leads to a changed life for Jesus.

THINK:

Why do you think that religious rules and practices are not needed to be saved?

GRACIOUS LIVING
Acts 15:22-35

The apostles, the elders and the rest of the church thought it a good idea to choose some people to go with Barnabas and Paul to Antioch. They sent Judas, who is also called Barsabbas, and Silas with them. These men were good leaders in the church in Jerusalem. They carried a letter with them. It read, '**Brethren**, from the apostles and elders of the church in Jerusalem, to the brethren who are Gentiles living in Antioch and Syria and Cilicia, greetings to you all. We have heard that some people who came from us, have greatly troubled you by their words. They have upset you by what they have said, even though we did not give them any instructions. We have come to one opinion, so we thought it good to choose some men and send them to you with our beloved Paul and Barnabas. These men have risked their lives in the service of our Lord Jesus Christ. Therefore, we have sent Judas and Silas along with them. They will tell you the same things that we are saying. It seemed good to the Holy Spirit and to us, that we should not burden you any further than these things: stay away from anything that has been sacrificed to an **idol**, from blood, from any animal that has been strangled, and from sexual immorality. It will be good for all of you to stay away from these things. Goodbye.'

Having been sent away, they went down to Antioch. Once there, they called the believers together and gave them the letter. When they read the letter, they were happy because they were encouraged by it. Judas and Silas were also prophets. They said many things that encouraged and strengthened the church. They spent a long time with the disciples in Antioch. Then Judas and Silas were sent back to Jerusalem in peace. Paul and Barnabas stayed in Antioch, and with many others, taught and preached the Word of the Lord there.

WHAT'S THE POINT:

The church in Jerusalem knew that the gospel of Jesus could change anyone, from every language and place. No one is greater than anyone else. The letter from Jerusalem to the Christians in Antioch said this was true. It also encouraged the new believers to live godly lives that glorified God because God had shown his grace to them. God's grace leads to a life of worship and purity and peace.

LOOK FORWARD:

Read Galatians 5:16-25

Real change comes from knowing Jesus – holding tightly on to Jesus – walking with Jesus every moment of every day – and receiving his wonderful and forgiving Holy Spirit.

THINK:

When you read the Bible, do you find it hard to listen to Jesus and do what he says all the time? If so, why?

THE SECOND MISSION
Acts 15:36 – 16:15

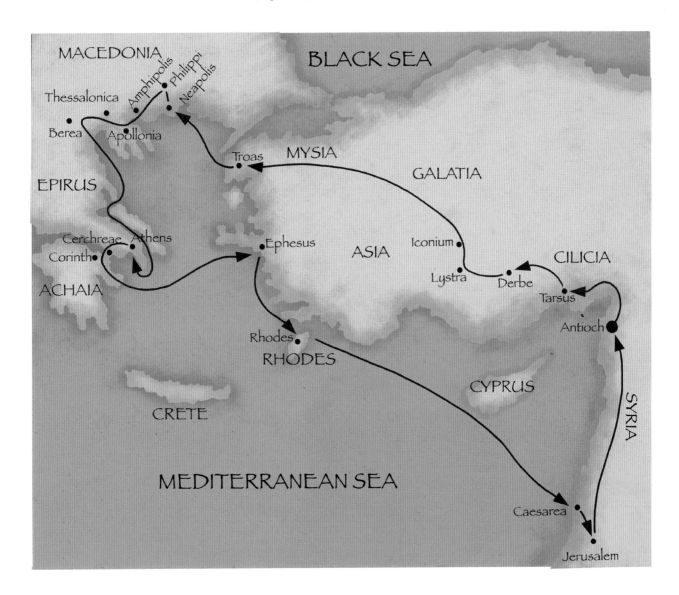

Some days later, Paul said to Barnabas, 'Let's go back and visit our brethren in all the cities where we preached the good news of the Lord. We can see how they are keeping.' Barnabas wanted to take John Mark with them. Paul was not so keen about that, as John Mark left them back in Pamphylia and did not help with the work. The disagreement was so bad that they went their separate ways. Barnabas took John Mark with him and sailed to Cyprus. Paul took Silas with him and travelled through Syria and Cilicia, and into the region of Galatia. They encouraged the churches in these places on the way. The churches grew in numbers every day.

Then they passed by Mysia and came to Troas. During the night, Paul had a vision. A man from Macedonia stood before him and begged, 'Come to Macedonia and help us.' After Paul had seen the vision, he left for Macedonia at once, along with Silas. They concluded that God wanted them to preach the gospel in Macedonia. Dr Luke also joined them on their journey.

From Troas, they travelled straight to Samothrace. The next day they went to Neapolis and then on to Philippi, which was the main city of that part of Macedonia. Philippi was also a Roman settlement. They stayed in that city for a number of days. One Sabbath, they went to a place of prayer which was outside the city gate. They sat by the side of the river and spoke to the women who were there. A woman from Thyatira listened very carefully to what Paul and the others were saying about Jesus. Her name was Lydia. She was a successful business woman who sold beautiful purple cloths. Lydia was also a God-fearing woman. The Lord helped her to understand what Paul was saying. God changed her sinful heart. She became a Christian, and was baptised, along with her household. Lydia insisted, 'If you consider me a true believer in the Lord, come and stay at my home.' And she persuaded the men to stay with her.

WHAT'S THE POINT:

After an argument, Paul and Barnabas parted company. God directed Paul and his travelling companions west to Macedonia. God wanted the good news to keep spreading to people who had never heard it before. When they arrived at Philippi they preached the gospel of Jesus Christ. God opened the hearts of people so that they believed in Jesus. God wants his message to spread and for us to tell others about Jesus. When we do, God opens their hearts to believe in Jesus.

THINK:

What part do you play in the salvation of other people? What part does God play?

WHO'S THE BOSS?

Acts 16:16-40

Paul and the others were going to the place of prayer. They were met by a servant girl who possessed a spirit that was able to tell fortunes. She had made her masters a lot of money doing it. She followed them and cried out, 'These men are the servants of the Most High God, who tell us the way of salvation.' She did this for many days. Paul became annoyed by this. He turned to the spirit and said, 'In the name of Jesus Christ, I command you, evil spirit, to come out of this girl.' And the spirit left her.

When her masters saw that their hope of making more money was gone, they grabbed Paul and Silas and hauled them

before the rulers of the city. They said, 'These men are Jews, and they are causing a lot of trouble in our city. They are teaching customs that are not lawful for us as Romans, to have or follow.'

The crowds also rose up against them. The rulers of the city tore their clothes and commanded that they be beaten with rods. After they were severely beaten, they were thrown into prison. The jailer was ordered to keep them securely locked up. So, he threw them into the inner prison and locked their feet in chains.

At midnight, Paul and Silas prayed and sang songs of praise to God. The other prisoners who were there heard them. Suddenly there was a huge earthquake. It shook the foundations of the prison. All of a sudden, the doors opened, and the shackles fell off. The prison jailer woke. He saw that the prison doors were opened. He thought that the prisoners had all escaped. The jailer drew his sword to kill himself, but Paul shouted at him. 'Do not hurt yourself. All of us are here!' The jailer called for lights. He ran into the prison cell. He was shaking with fear, and he threw himself onto the ground, right in front of Paul and Silas. The jailer got up and brought the men out of the prison cell. 'Sirs, what must I do to be saved?' he asked.

'Believe in the Lord Jesus Christ and you will be saved, you and your household,' they replied. They spoke the Word of the Lord to him and to everyone in his house. That very hour, the jailor took them and washed their wounds. He and his family were baptised immediately. Then the jailor took the men to his home and fed them. And he was glad that he and his family now believed in the Lord.

Night turned to day and the rulers of the city sent the police to the jailor with a message. 'Let those men go,' they said. The jailor went to Paul and said, 'The rulers of the city have ordered your release. You can leave. Go in peace.' But Paul said, 'They have beaten us openly, even though we were not guilty of anything. We are citizens of Rome, and they threw us into prison. And now they want to throw us out of the city in secret? No way! Let the rulers come here and escort us out.'

The police officers told the city rulers everything that Paul said to them. When they heard that the men were citizens of Rome, they got scared. They went to Paul and Silas and begged for their forgiveness and asked them to leave Philippi. So, they left the prison and went to see Lydia and the other believers. After they encouraged them, Paul and Silas left the city.

WHAT'S THE POINT:

Paul and his companions often found that people were against them. But when it looked like everything had gone wrong, God changed things. God is in control. God is the boss. God will make sure the gospel of his Son Jesus carries on, even when there is hostility against his people.

LOOK FORWARD:

Read 1 John 3:8

Jesus came into the world to conquer the work of Satan by dying on the cross and rising from the dead. He did this so that we can become children of God. Jesus wins, no matter what!

THINK:

In what ways are you encouraged by the examples of Paul and Silas?

BE LIKE A BEREAN!
Acts 17:1-15

Paul and Silas passed through Amphipolis and Apollonia. They arrived at Thessalonica. There was a Jewish synagogue there and Paul went in. He usually did that when he arrived at a new place. Over three Sabbaths, Paul spoke from the Scriptures in order to explain and convince the people of the importance of Christ's death and resurrection. He said to them, 'This Jesus, the one that I am telling you all about, is the Christ.' Some of the Jews were convinced and they joined Paul and Silas. Some of the God-fearing Greeks also believed and so did a number of prominent women in the city. But there were Jews that did not believe Paul's message. They were envious of Paul and Silas. They gathered some wicked men together and formed a mob. They went through the city and started a riot. They attacked the house of a man called Jason, because they thought Paul and Silas were there. They wanted to bring the men out to the people. But they could not find them. So, they grabbed Jason and some other disciples of Jesus, and hauled them before the rulers of the city. 'These men have turned the world upside down!' they shouted. 'And now they have come here to our city. This man, Jason, opened his home to them. All of them are breaking the commands of Caesar. They say there is another king. His name is Jesus.'

The rulers and people of the city were greatly upset when they heard these things. Once Jason and the others paid a fine, they were released.

During the night, the disciples sent Paul and Silas away to the city of Berea, in the south of Macedonia. When they got there, the men went into the synagogue of the Jews. The people there were more dignified than those in Thessalonica. They were keen to hear the Word of God. Every day they searched the Scriptures to make sure that Paul and Silas were preaching the truth. Many placed their trust in Jesus as Saviour and King. But the unbelieving Jews from Thessalonica heard that Paul and Silas were preaching the Word of God in Berea. So they travelled to Berea and stirred up the people against Paul and Silas. At once, the believers there sent Paul away to the seaside. However, Silas, and a man called Timothy, stayed in Berea. Paul's travelling companions took him to Athens. Paul told them to go back to Berea and instruct Silas and Timothy to join him as soon as possible. Once they had received this instruction, the men left him.

WHAT'S THE POINT:

Paul taught the Thessalonians and the Bereans from the Bible. It was misunderstood on purpose, and it produced a violent response in Thessalonica. However, Paul's preaching was eagerly received by many in Berea. They checked everything Paul said with the Scriptures to make sure he was telling them the truth about the Lord. The Bereans really wanted to hear and learn the truth about God. We should be like the Bereans!

LOOK FORWARD:

Read 2 Timothy 3:16-17

From his conversion, Paul believed in the complete authority of God's Word. The Scriptures were at the heart of his ministry. That is why he spent all his time preaching and teaching the Bible to everyone.

THINK:

When you read the Bible and it says something that challenges you, what do you do?

THE TRUE AND LIVING GOD

Acts 17:16-34

Paul waited for Silas and Timothy in Athens. Meanwhile, he walked about the city and saw that it was full of statues of idols. It made him sick to his stomach. As usual, Paul went into the synagogue and debated with the Jews and those who were God-fearers. He even went into the marketplace every day to proclaim the gospel to any who would listen. Epicurean and Stoic philosophers also debated with Paul. Some of them said, 'What is this man babbling on about?' Others said, 'He seems to be promoting foreign gods.' They said this because Paul was preaching about Jesus and that he had risen from the dead. They took Paul to the council of the **Areopagus**. 'May we know more about this new teaching that you are presenting us with?' they asked. 'You are saying some strange things. We would like to know what they mean.' The Athenians and foreigners who lived in the city loved to spend their time discussing new things.

TO AN UNKNOWN GOD

Paul stood in the midst of the Areopagus and said, 'People of Athens. I can see that in every way, you are very religious. As I walked along your streets, I saw many objects of your devotion. I even found an altar with the words, "To an unknown god" written on it. You worship an unknown god, but I am going to tell you all about him. The God who made the world and everything in it is the Lord of heaven and earth. He does not live in temples that have been built by human hands. He does not need to be served by our hands as if he needed anything. Rather, he is the God who gives us life. He gives us every breath. He gives us everything that we have. From one man, God made every nation to live together in this world. He decided when and where they should live. He did this so that they would look for him and draw close to him and find him. In fact, God is near us, just as one of your philosophers said, "In him we live and move and exist." Even one of your poets declared, "For we are his children."

'As we are God's children, we ought not to think that God is like gold, or silver, or stone that can be made into a statue using our imagination and hands. God took no notice of humanity's ignorance in the past. But now he commands all people, everyone, everywhere, to repent. Turn from your sin! God has set a day when he will judge the world by the man whom he has appointed. So that all people may know this to be true, God has raised this man from the dead.'

Some of the people poked fun at Paul when he talked about the resurrection from the dead. But others said to him, 'We want to hear more of this message.' When Paul left them, there were some who went with him. They believed the gospel of Jesus, repented of their sins, and put their faith in Jesus. A man called Dionysius was one of them. He was a member of the Areopagus. Another was a woman called Damaris. It was a wonderful day for them!

WHAT'S THE POINT:

The people of Athens believed in many gods. But they did not know the one true and living God. Therefore, Paul told them what God is like. God calls people everywhere to stop following false gods. They must turn back to him and repent. God has fixed a day when he will judge the world with justice. God has appointed Jesus to be our judge. We know this is true because God has raised Jesus from the dead. The resurrection of Jesus is the proof that Judgement Day is coming. So, repent!

LOOK BACK:

Read Matthew 25:1-13

One unpredictable day Jesus will come again. Make sure you are ready to meet him face to face!

CHECK THIS OUT:

Read 1 Corinthians 15:1-8 and 12-22

What we believe about the resurrection of Jesus will determine whether we stand as Christians or fall away from the truth of the gospel.

THINK:

Is there anything that you cannot live without? Be careful of idolatry.

TO AN
UNKNOWN
GOD

FEAR NOT

Acts 18:1-17

Paul left Athens and went on to Corinth. He stayed at the home of Aquila and Priscilla. They were tentmakers, just like Paul. They worked together in the city making tents. Every Sabbath, Paul went into the synagogue to tell the Jews and God-fearing Greeks about Jesus.

Soon after, Silas and Timothy arrived from Macedonia. Paul was still witnessing to the Jews that Jesus is the Christ. But they were against Paul, and they hated him. As they opposed the good news of Jesus, Paul decided that he would bring the gospel to the Gentiles instead. He left the synagogue and went next door to the home of a God-fearing man called Titius Justus. The ruler of the synagogue was called Crispus. He and his family believed in the Lord. In fact, many of the Corinthian people believed and were baptised.

One night, the Lord appeared to Paul in a vision. The Lord said to Paul, 'Do not be afraid to keep on telling people about me. I am with you Paul. No one will hurt you. I have many people in this city.' So, Paul decided to stay in Corinth for a year and a half. During that time, he kept on teaching the Word of God.

The Jews continued to make trouble for Paul. They brought him to the authorities and tried to have him punished for telling people about God. They accused Paul of trying to convince the people to disobey God's Law. But the leader, Gallio, was not interested in their squabbles. As Paul had not committed any crime, Gallio told the Jews to sort it out themselves. He made them leave. On the way out, they grabbed the ruler of the synagogue, Sosthenes, and beat him up. Gallio ignored everything that happened.

WHAT'S THE POINT:

God had many people in Corinth who were ready to believe and follow Jesus once they heard the gospel from Paul and his companions. God encouraged Paul to stay in the city. He protected him from harm, so that Paul could keep on speaking about Jesus. Don't be afraid. The gospel has the power to save people, even though many reject it. You never know what unlikely person will be saved next!

LOOK BACK:

Read Ezekiel 33:7-9

We do not have the same responsibility as the apostle Paul and the prophet Ezekiel, but all disciples of Jesus are his witnesses in the world.

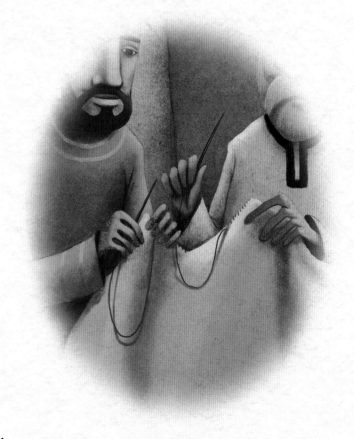

THINK:

Can you think of a time when you had the **chance** to tell someone about Jesus, but you didn't take it? How does that make you feel?

THE THIRD MISSION
Acts 18:18 – 19:7

Paul set sail for Syria. Priscilla and Aquila travelled with him. They came to Ephesus and Paul left Priscilla and Aquila there to encourage the church. As usual, Paul went into the synagogue to debate with the Jews that Jesus is the **Messiah**. They wanted Paul to stay with them a while longer, but he refused. Then he said to them, 'I will come back to you if God wants me to.' With that, he left Ephesus by boat.

At Caesarea Paul stepped off the boat. He went to the church in that city to see the disciples. He wanted to encourage them to keep following the Lord. Not long after, Paul went down to Antioch. He spent some time in that city before heading on to the region

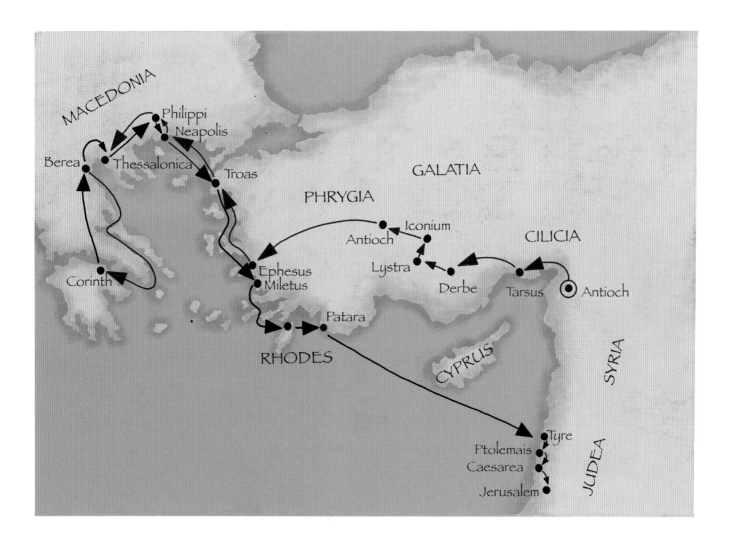

of Galatia and Phrygia. He went from place to place encouraging the disciples to keep their trust in the Lord and strengthening their faith with the Word of God.

At that time, a Jewish man from Alexandria came to Ephesus. His name was Apollos. He was a fine speaker, and he knew the Scriptures well. He had been taught the Christian faith. Apollos was keen to speak and clearly teach the good news about Jesus. So, he went to the synagogue and started to preach about Jesus. Priscilla and Aquila were there, and they heard Apollos speak. They decided to take him home. They took time to explain the gospel of Jesus clearly to him. Apollos wanted to travel to the region of Achaia. The disciples in Ephesus encouraged him to go there. They wrote to the believers in Achaia asking that Apollos be warmly welcomed. When Apollos got there, he helped those who, by the grace of God, believed in Jesus. He debated with the Jews and showed them from the Scriptures that Jesus is the Christ.

At the same time that Apollos was in Corinth, Paul travelled inland to Ephesus. He found some disciples of John the Baptist in that city. There were about twelve of them. 'Did you receive the Holy Spirit when you became believers?' Paul asked them.

'No, we didn't,' they replied. 'We didn't even know that there was a Holy Spirit!' they exclaimed.

'What baptism did you have?' asked Paul.

'The baptism of John the Baptist,' they said.

'Ah yes,' said Paul. 'John's was a baptism of repentance. John told the people to believe in the man who would come after him. He wanted everyone to believe in Jesus.'

When they heard this, they believed and were baptised in the name of the Lord Jesus. Then Paul laid his hands on them, and the Holy Spirit came upon them. They started to speak the Word of God in other languages that were not their own.

WHAT'S THE POINT:

The Ephesians knew something about Jesus. But they did not know the whole story. They needed to be taught the gospel clearly and that is what Paul did. Apollos had been taught the Christian faith. But he needed Priscilla and Aquila to explain it more fully. Many people know something about Jesus, but they need to hear the whole truth about Jesus. We need to have the Bible taught to us. And we need faithful teachers who can do that well.

LOOK BACK:

Read Luke 3:3-17 and John 5:35-36

John the Baptist knew that people needed to repent from sin and turn back to God. He knew that Jesus was God's promised Messiah. But he didn't know all the details about how God would bring that about. Those who were baptised in the name of John needed to repent of their sins and be baptised in the name of Jesus Christ for eternal life.

CHECK THIS OUT:

Read Romans 12:4-8

A body has parts that work together to make it function properly. It is like that with the church, when people work together for the good of the gospel.

THINK:

The Holy Spirit did not come upon the men until Paul laid his hands on them. Why do you think it happened in this unusual way?

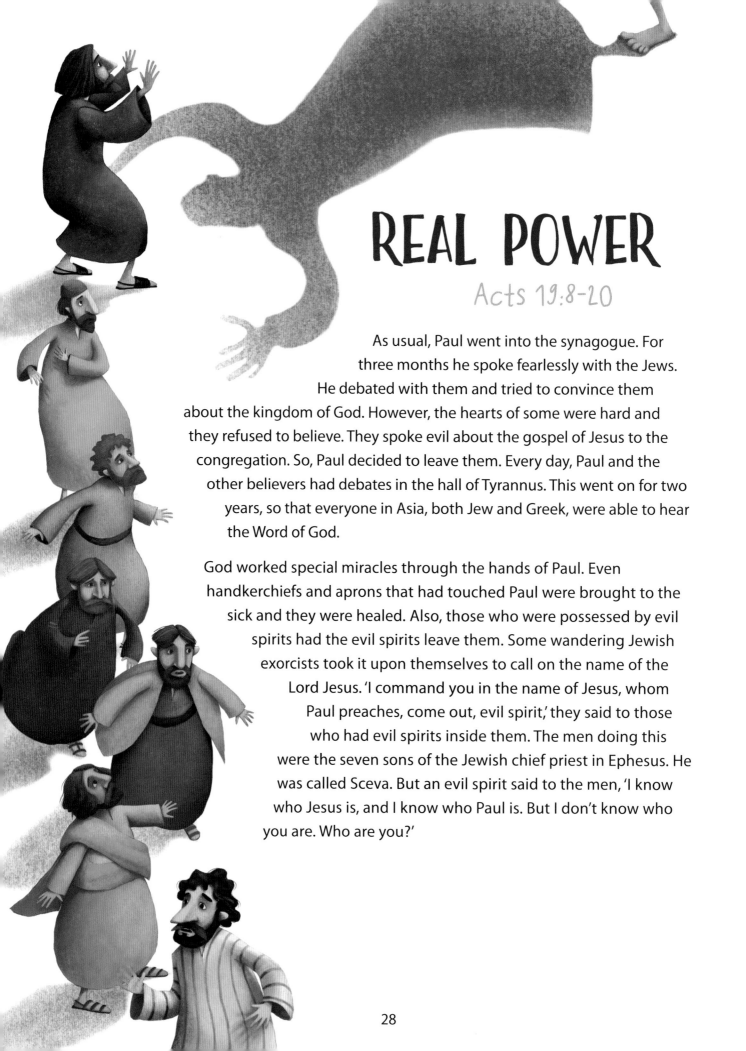

REAL POWER

Acts 19:8-20

As usual, Paul went into the synagogue. For three months he spoke fearlessly with the Jews. He debated with them and tried to convince them about the kingdom of God. However, the hearts of some were hard and they refused to believe. They spoke evil about the gospel of Jesus to the congregation. So, Paul decided to leave them. Every day, Paul and the other believers had debates in the hall of Tyrannus. This went on for two years, so that everyone in Asia, both Jew and Greek, were able to hear the Word of God.

God worked special miracles through the hands of Paul. Even handkerchiefs and aprons that had touched Paul were brought to the sick and they were healed. Also, those who were possessed by evil spirits had the evil spirits leave them. Some wandering Jewish exorcists took it upon themselves to call on the name of the Lord Jesus. 'I command you in the name of Jesus, whom Paul preaches, come out, evil spirit,' they said to those who had evil spirits inside them. The men doing this were the seven sons of the Jewish chief priest in Ephesus. He was called Sceva. But an evil spirit said to the men, 'I know who Jesus is, and I know who Paul is. But I don't know who you are. Who are you?'

Just then the man in whom the evil spirit lived, jumped on the sons of Sceva. Using violence, the possessed man overpowered them. They ran from the house as fast as they could. They were injured and their clothes were torn off.

Everyone in Ephesus heard about this and they were afraid. The name of the Lord Jesus was worshipped. And many that believed came and confessed openly what they had done. Some who practised magic gathered their books together and burned them before the people. They worked out how much the books cost and discovered it came to about fifty thousand **silver pieces**. The Word of God continued to grow and triumph over evil.

WHAT'S THE POINT:

Dark magic was everywhere in Ephesus. People valued 'power' no matter where it came from. They thought Paul's 'magic' was more powerful than any they had seen before. They knew that Paul drove out evil spirits in the name of Jesus. The Jewish sons of Sceva tried to copy him, even though they did not know Jesus as Lord and Saviour themselves. Others repented and believed in Jesus. They got rid of their magic books. They knew that they had to change and turn away from evil things. The gospel changes people, as they believe in Jesus as Saviour and obey him as Lord.

LOOK FORWARD:

Read 2 Corinthians 5:17 and Ephesians 4:17-24

The gospel of Jesus changes people. The old life that once loved sin is gone. There is a new life instead!

THINK:

Does your life show that the gospel of Jesus has changed you?

ANOTHER RIOT

Acts 19:21-41

After all these things had happened and under the guidance of the Holy Spirit, Paul travelled through Macedonia and Achaia. He was on his way to Jerusalem. He said to the disciples in Ephesus, 'After I visit Jerusalem, I must travel on to Rome.' He sent two helpers, Timothy, and Erastus, on to Macedonia ahead of him. Paul remained in Asia a while longer.

There was uproar in Ephesus because of the Way of the Lord. A silversmith called Demetrius made silver shrines of the temple of Artemis. He attracted plenty of business for the other skilled workers in the city. He called all the skilled workers and craftsmen together and said to them, 'Men, you all know that our wealth comes from this work. All of you can see and hear what Paul has done in Ephesus and even throughout Asia. He has persuaded and turned away a great number of people, telling them that man-made gods are no gods at all! Not only is our craft in danger, the temple of our great goddess Artemis is in danger of being despised. Her majesty is in danger of being overthrown – the goddess who is worshipped not only in Asia, but in the whole world.'

The people were angry when they heard this and they shouted, 'Great is Artemis of the Ephesians!' The whole city was in uproar. They grabbed Paul's friends, Gaius, and Aristarchus. As the mob rushed into the theatre, the two men were dragged in with them. Paul wanted to go among the crowd, but the disciples would not let him. Some of his friends, who were members of the local authorities, sent word to Paul, begging him not to go in to the theatre. The assembly was confused. Some

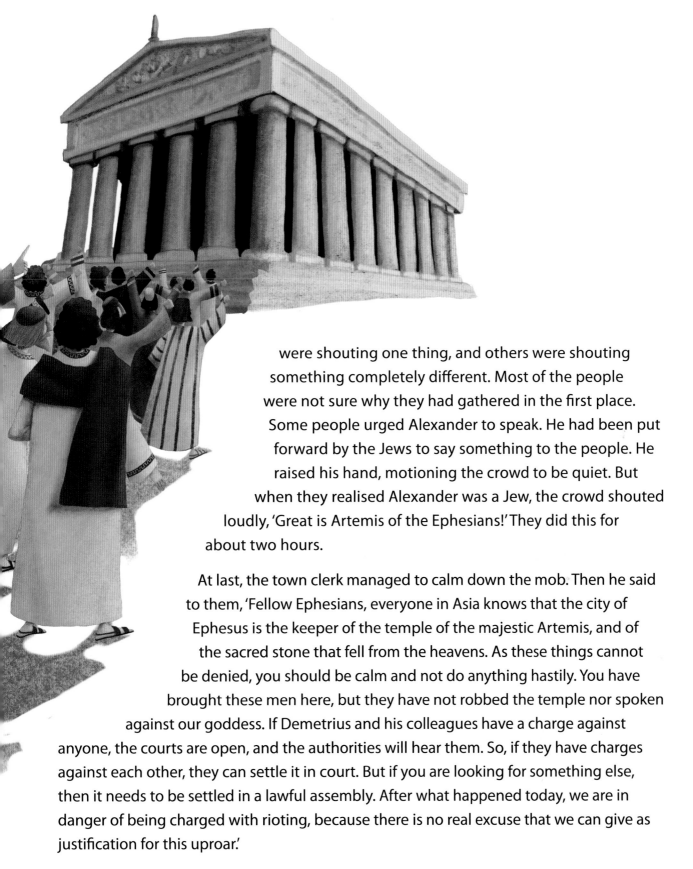

were shouting one thing, and others were shouting something completely different. Most of the people were not sure why they had gathered in the first place. Some people urged Alexander to speak. He had been put forward by the Jews to say something to the people. He raised his hand, motioning the crowd to be quiet. But when they realised Alexander was a Jew, the crowd shouted loudly, 'Great is Artemis of the Ephesians!' They did this for about two hours.

At last, the town clerk managed to calm down the mob. Then he said to them, 'Fellow Ephesians, everyone in Asia knows that the city of Ephesus is the keeper of the temple of the majestic Artemis, and of the sacred stone that fell from the heavens. As these things cannot be denied, you should be calm and not do anything hastily. You have brought these men here, but they have not robbed the temple nor spoken against our goddess. If Demetrius and his colleagues have a charge against anyone, the courts are open, and the authorities will hear them. So, if they have charges against each other, they can settle it in court. But if you are looking for something else, then it needs to be settled in a lawful assembly. After what happened today, we are in danger of being charged with rioting, because there is no real excuse that we can give as justification for this uproar.'

When the town clerk said these things, he sent the crowd away.

WHAT'S THE POINT:

The gospel of Jesus had changed Ephesus. Many people stopped worshipping false gods. They now worshipped the only true God. Those who rejected the gospel of Jesus were angry because of the change that was happening in the city. It was having a bad impact on their income. Anger led to rioting. Once again, the apostle Paul was in danger. When the gospel changes lives those who believe in Jesus can be in danger from others who refuse to change for the sake of Jesus.

LOOK BACK:

Read John 15:18-20 and John 16:33

The world loves its own kind. It does not *hate* Jesus and *love* his disciples. If you are different because you love and obey Jesus, you will be hated too. Sad, but true. However, take heart because Jesus has overcome the world!

CHECK THIS OUT:

Read 1 Timothy 6:6-10

The love of money brought evil to Ephesus. The love of money still threatens the work of the gospel today. Can you think of ways that it does?

THINK:

Can you think of countries in the world that **persecute** and kill people for being Christians? Pray that God would give his people in those countries strength and courage to be faithful to Jesus.

ENCOURAGEMENT

Acts 20:1-12

When the riot in Ephesus stopped, Paul called the disciples to him. He spent some time encouraging them and then left for Macedonia. As he was going through the region, Paul encouraged the disciples that he met along the way. Then he arrived in Greece and spent three months there. He learned that the Jews were plotting against him just as he was ready to sail to Syria. So, Paul decided to go back through Macedonia instead. Others went with him on his journey. Eventually they arrived in Troas, where they remained for seven days.

The disciples came together on the first day of the week to break bread. It was the day before Paul's departure from Troas. Paul preached the Word of God to them. He spoke for a long time until midnight. There were many lights in the upper room where they met. In one window sat a young man called Eutychus, whose name means 'fortunate'. He fell into a deep

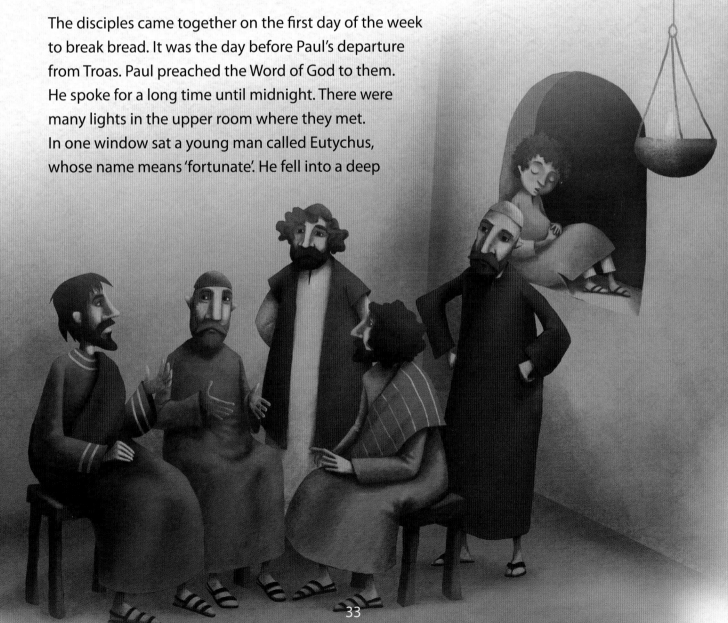

sleep as Paul kept talking. Then he fell out of the window and landed on the ground three storeys below! Some came to his aid, but then saw he was dead.

Paul ran down the stairs as quickly as he could. He bent over and took Eutychus in his arms. He said, 'Do not be alarmed, he is still alive!' Then Paul went back upstairs to eat with the disciples. He talked with them until dawn, and then he left them. They took the fortunate young man home alive, and they were greatly comforted.

WHAT'S THE POINT:

Paul strengthened the disciples he met by encouraging them from God's Word. When Paul raised Eutychus back to life, the disciples were greatly encouraged too. The miracle reminded them that death is not the end for anyone who believes in Jesus. Encouragement is important. We all need it. We all need to give it. It helps us keep going as Christians, even when things are tough.

LOOK BACK:

Read 1 Kings 17:17-24

The prophet Elijah was God's messenger. He spoke the words of the Lord. Those who listened were strengthened and encouraged to love and follow God.

THINK:

Can you think of a Christian friend to encourage in the next few days?

SETTING A GOOD EXAMPLE
Acts 20:13-38

Paul wanted to be in Jerusalem for the Feast of **Pentecost**. He left Troas on foot, heading to the city of Assos. His companions sailed to Assos instead and met Paul there. When they were all together, Paul jumped aboard the ship, and they sailed along the coast, stopping at Mitylene, Chios, and Samos until they reached Miletus. He sent a message to the leaders of the church at Ephesus to join him in Miletus.

When they arrived, he said to them, 'You all know that from the moment I arrived in Asia, I have not stopped serving the Lord. I did so humbly and with tears due to the hard times that I experienced at the hands of the Jews who were against me. I taught you everything that would be helpful to you, and I did this in public as well as in your homes. I warned both the Jews and the Gentiles that they should turn away from their sins. I would rather they turn back to God and believe in his Son, the Lord Jesus Christ. And now I am going to Jerusalem in obedience to the Holy Spirit. I do not know what will happen to me there. The Holy Spirit has told me that in every city I visit, there is nothing but hardship and imprisonment that awaits me. My life is of no value to me. All I want is to finish the course and the work that the Lord has given to me. I want to tell everyone the good news of the grace of God. Those of you who heard me proclaim the kingdom of God in Ephesus will never see me again. I told you everything about God's plan and purpose, so I am not accountable for those of you who refuse to believe. Therefore, look after yourselves and watch over the flock that the Holy Spirit has given you to care for. Be shepherds of God's church which he bought with his own blood shed on the cross. When I leave you, I know that fierce wolves will come among you. They will not spare the flock. There will be some from among your own number who will say things to draw disciples away from Christ. So, watch out! Remember that every day for three years I did not stop instructing each of you with tears. Now, I entrust you to God's care and to the message of his grace. It can build you up and

give you the **inheritance** which is received by those who belong to God and live holy lives. I did not want anyone's silver or gold or clothing. You know for yourselves that these hands of mine worked hard to provide everything that I and my companions needed. In this way I have shown you that by working hard in all things, we must help those who are weak. We must remember the words of the Lord Jesus who said, "It is more blessed to give than to receive."'

When Paul had finished talking, he knelt down and prayed with them. Everyone cried and hugged Paul and kissed him. They were very sad, because Paul said that they would not see him again. Then they went with him to the ship and said goodbye.

WHAT'S THE POINT:

A few years earlier, Paul started the church in Ephesus through preaching the gospel of Jesus. As Paul was heading to Jerusalem and on to Rome, he called the Ephesian leaders together. He wanted to urge them to keep looking after themselves and God's people. Church leaders are responsible for looking after Christians. They must teach God's Word faithfully. They must defend against false teachers. They must model a godly lifestyle.

LOOK BACK:

Read John 10:11-15

The ultimate safety of those who trust in Jesus rests with Jesus. He is the Good Shepherd who cares for his sheep: those who believe in him. He gives those who believe in him, other shepherds to care for them and protect them from danger.

LOOK FORWARD:

Read Revelation 2:1-7

This is what Jesus thinks about the Ephesian church roughly fifty years after Paul spoke to its leaders in Miletus. What is good, and what is bad in this letter?

CHECK THIS OUT:

Read Philippians 3:17-19

God's Word is the great weapon against false teaching. Read it carefully and know what it says. Remember to be like the Bereans!

THINK:

Do you pray for your leaders at church? If not, start today! They need God's grace as they look after God's people in their care.

BE READY
Acts 21:1-16

Paul and his companions sailed along the coast to Cos, then Rhodes and then Patara. They stopped in each place for only a day. They sailed on to Syria and landed at Tyre. The next day they came to Ptolemais and the day after that, they arrived in Caesarea. They stayed at the home of an evangelist called Philip. Back in Jerusalem, Philip was chosen as one of the seven helpers, along with Stephen. Philip had four daughters who were not married. They loved to tell people the good news of Jesus. While Paul and his friends were staying with Philip, a prophet called Agabus came down from Judea to visit them. Agabus took Paul's belt, and he tied his own hands and feet with it.

'This is what the Holy Spirit says,' Agabus said. 'The man who owns this belt will be bound in the same way by the Jews in Jerusalem and handed over to the Gentiles.' When they heard these words, they begged Paul not to go to Jerusalem.

'What are you doing?' asked Paul. 'You are breaking my heart with all this weeping,' he said. 'I am ready to go to prison and even die in Jerusalem for the name of our Lord Jesus,' said Paul.

As no one could change Paul's mind, his friends said to him, 'May the Lord's will be done.'

Soon after, Paul and his companions went up to Jerusalem. Some disciples from Caesarea went with them. They all stayed at the home of a man called Mnason. He was from Cyprus and was an early disciple of the Lord Jesus.

WHAT'S THE POINT:

Paul is on his way to Jerusalem. He knew that he would suffer there for his faith in Jesus. Again and again the believers begged him not to go to Jerusalem. However, Paul was unwavering. He was willing to suffer and die for the Lord Jesus. Christians are called to follow Jesus, whatever the cost.

LOOK BACK:

Read Mark 8:34-38

Jesus calls his disciples to deny themselves, take up their cross and follow him. Even if that means suffering for him. Even if that means dying for him. Are you prepared for that?

THINK:

You may not face prison or death for being a Christian. What challenges and sacrifices are you facing today?

WRONGLY ACCUSED

Acts 21:17-36

Paul and the others were welcomed by the followers of Jesus in Jerusalem. He visited the apostle James and the other elders of the church. Paul told them everything that the Lord had done among the Gentiles through his ministry. They gave thanks to God when they heard his report.

'There have also been many thousands of Jews who have believed in the Lord Jesus here in Jerusalem,' they said. 'They are devoted to the Law of Moses as well. They have heard of you, Paul. They have been told that you teach the Jews who live in Gentile regions to forget about the Law of Moses; that they should not circumcise their children, nor pay attention to our traditions. No doubt they will learn of your presence here in Jerusalem. Therefore, this is what we want you to do. There are four men here who have taken an oath. Go with them and join in the service of purification with them. Pay their expenses, so that they can have their heads shaved. This will let the people know that there is no truth in any of the things they have heard about you. Rather, they will see that you too observe the Law of Moses. We have sent a letter to the Gentiles who believe in the Lord. We said that in our judgement, they should not eat any food that has been offered to idols, or any blood, or animals that have been strangled. They should also keep themselves from sexual sins.'

The next day Paul took the men with him. They purified themselves and went into the Jewish temple so that they could announce when their purification would end. At that point an offering would be made for each of them.

When the seven days were almost done, some Jews from Asia saw Paul in the temple. They provoked the people to anger. They grabbed Paul, shouting out, 'Fellow Jews, help us! This is the man who is teaching everyone the world over, to go against the people of Israel, the Law of Moses, and the temple. Not only that, but he has also brought some Gentiles into the temple and has made it unclean!' They said this because they had seen Trophimus from Ephesus with Paul in Jerusalem. They assumed that Paul had brought him into the temple.

The whole city was in an uproar. The people ran together and seized Paul. They dragged him out of the temple and the doors closed straight away. As they were about to kill him, the commander of the Roman soldiers learned that all of Jerusalem was in uproar. He immediately took some officers and soldiers and ran down to the temple. When Paul's enemies saw the commander and soldiers coming, they stopped beating him.

The commander came up to Paul and arrested him. He ordered that Paul be bound by two chains. He asked Paul who he was and what he had done to make the crowd so angry.

Some began to shout one thing while others shouted something completely different. Due to the confusion, the commander could not find out exactly what happened. Therefore, he ordered that Paul be taken to the **garrison**. When Paul arrived there he had to be carried up the steps by the soldiers because of the violent beating he had received. The crowd followed the soldiers, shouting loudly, 'Get rid of him!'

WHAT'S THE POINT:

Paul was wrongly accused of telling Jewish believers to forget about their traditions and culture. He was also accused of bringing a Greek man into a Jewish temple. However, they made a big mistake. Paul respected people and always tried to live at peace with everyone. He longed for them to hear the gospel of Jesus and be saved. But not everyone welcomed the good news from Paul. The Jews made up false charges against Paul, so that they could kill him. Does that sound familiar?

LOOK FORWARD:

Read 1 Corinthians 9:22

Paul became like a Jew to win the Jews. The purification service didn't matter to Paul. But if it helped to overcome narrow-mindedness, Paul was willing to do it. He just wanted to win the Jews round, so that they would listen to him speak about Jesus the Messiah and be saved.

CHECK THIS OUT:

Read Romans 12:17-21

Throughout Paul's missionary journeys, he practised what he preached. It was no different in Jerusalem.

THINK:

Do you think there is a difference between being *religious* and *following Jesus*? If so, what?

EARS THAT DO NOT HEAR

Acts 21:37 – 22:29

As Paul was being led into the garrison, he spoke to the Roman commander. 'May I say something to you?' he asked. 'You can speak Greek?' replied the commander in surprise. 'Are you not that Egyptian who caused a riot and led about four thousand terrorists out into the wilderness a while back?' he asked.

'No, I am a Jewish man from Tarsus in Cilicia,' answered Paul. 'I am a citizen of no ordinary city. Will you please let me speak to the people?'

The commander gave Paul permission to address the crowd. Paul stood on the steps. He motioned with his hand for the crowd to be calm. When there was silence, he began to speak to them in Aramaic.

'Fellow Israelites. Please listen to my defence that I now make to you all.' When they heard that Paul spoke to them in Aramaic, a great silence came upon them. 'I am truly a Jew. I was born in Tarsus, a city in Cilicia. But I was brought up here in Jerusalem. I was educated at the feet of Gamaliel and taught according to the strictness of the laws of our ancestors. I was very dedicated to God as all of you are here today.

'I afflicted death on those who followed the **Way**. I had men and women arrested and put in prison. The high priest and members of the council can testify that

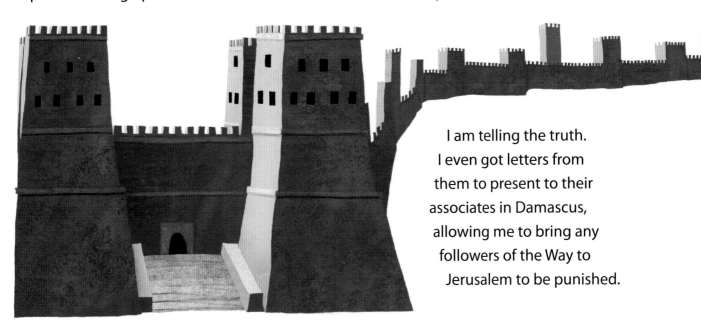

I am telling the truth. I even got letters from them to present to their associates in Damascus, allowing me to bring any followers of the Way to Jerusalem to be punished.

Paul then spoke of his conversion to Christ and his baptism. He told them of his presence at the death of Stephen in Jerusalem. He spoke of how the Lord had commanded him to leave Jerusalem. 'Go,' the Lord said to me, 'for I will send you far away, to the Gentiles.'

The people listened up to this point. But then they started to cry out, 'Kill this man! Wipe out his existence from the earth!' As they shouted out, they cast off their cloaks and threw dust into the air. The Roman commander ordered that Paul be brought into the garrison. He commanded that Paul be **flogged** and questioned, to find out why the crowd was against him.

However, when they had tied him up to be flogged, Paul said to the officer standing near him, 'Is it lawful for you to torture a Roman citizen who hasn't even been found guilty of a crime?' When the officer heard this, he went quickly to the commander and told him. 'What are you going to do?' he asked the commander. 'This man is a Roman citizen.'

So, the commander went to Paul. 'Is it true, are you a Roman citizen?' he asked Paul.

'Yes, I am,' answered Paul.

'I had to pay a lot of money to be a Roman citizen,' said the commander.

'But I was born a Roman citizen,' Paul replied.

Those who were about to question Paul left at once. Even the commander was alarmed when he realised that he had put Paul, a Roman citizen, in chains.

WHAT'S THE POINT:

Paul was once guilty of opposing the Messiah, Jesus. But he met Jesus, admitted his guilt, and was pardoned. The crowd could be pardoned too, if only they would listen to Paul's message. The garrison commander was frustrated. He didn't speak Aramaic and did not know what was being said. He wanted to flog Paul and find out the truth. Then Paul used his worldly privilege as a Roman citizen for Jesus. The gospel would go to the heart of the Roman empire, just as God promised.

THINK:

Paul took Jesus and the gospel seriously. How seriously do you take Jesus and his gospel? Or are you only serious about Jesus on Sundays?

FIGHT VALIANTLY

Acts 22:30 – 23:11

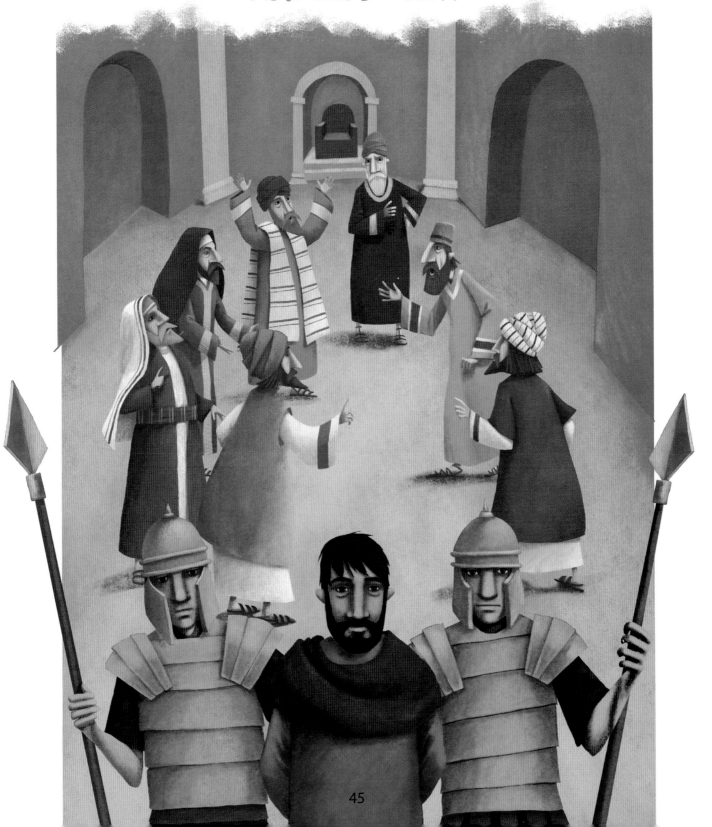

The Roman commander wanted to know the real reason why Paul was being accused by the Jews. He loosened his restraints and ordered the chief priests and the whole council to meet together. Then he brought Paul before them. Paul looked at them closely then said, 'Fellow Israelites. My conscience is clear concerning how I have lived before God to this very day.'

The high priest who was called Ananias, ordered the men standing beside Paul to smack him in the mouth. Paul said to Ananias, 'God will strike you also, you whitewashed wall! Are you going to judge me according to the law, and yet you break the law by telling them to hit me?'

The men standing near Paul said, 'Are you really going to abuse God's high priest?'

'I did not know that he was the high priest,' replied Paul. 'The Scripture says, "Do not speak evil of the ruler of your people."'

Paul looked around at the council. He saw that some members of the council were Sadducees, and others were Pharisees. He cried out, 'Brethren, I am a Pharisee – the son of Pharisees! I have been put on trial because of the hope I have in the dead rising to life again!'

When he said this, a dispute broke out between the Pharisees and the Sadducees, and they were divided. The Sadducees said that people will not rise from the dead. They also said that angels and spirits do not exist. However, the Pharisees believed in all of them. The shouting grew louder. Some of the scribes who belonged to the group of Pharisees strongly argued: 'We cannot find anything wrong in this man! Perhaps an angel or a spirit really did speak to him?'

The divisions became so violent that the Roman commander feared for Paul's safety. He ordered his soldiers to go into the meeting and remove Paul from them, by force if necessary. Then they took Paul back into the garrison.

The next night, the Lord said to Paul, 'Do not fear. You have been my witness in Jerusalem, and you will be my witness in Rome.'

WHAT'S THE POINT:

Paul did not defend any sinful practice in his ministry. His conscience was clear. He spoke the truth plainly, (just like Jesus did to the religious people of his day in Matthew 23:27). He repented the moment he realised he went against Scripture. And he sought out some common ground with the Pharisees on the resurrection. This is a great example of how to live as a Christian in controversial days.

LOOK FORWARD:

Read Jude 3

In every generation, God's people must contend for the truth of the gospel against those who oppose it.

THINK:

How does this passage in Acts encourage your trust in God? Read Romans 8:28 to help you further.

TRUST GOD

Acts 23:12-35

The next day, Paul's enemies plotted to murder him. They swore an oath, not to eat or drink until they had killed him. There were over forty of them. They went to the Jewish chief priests and elders to tell them of their plan. 'We have vowed together not to eat anything until we have killed Paul. We want you and the council to send word to the Roman commander to bring Paul down to you. Explain that you wish to examine his case more closely. We will be ready to kill Paul before he gets here.'

Paul's nephew learned of the plot. He went to the garrison and told Paul. Then Paul called for one of the officers to come to him. 'Take this young man to the commander. He has something to tell him,' said Paul. The officer brought him to the commander who asked the young man, 'What do you have to tell me?'

'The Jewish authorities will ask you to bring Paul down to the council tomorrow,' said the young man. 'They will give the impression that they want to examine his case more closely. But do not give in to them. More than forty of them are lying in wait to kill him. They have sworn an oath not to eat or drink anything until they have killed Paul. They are ready to do it and are waiting for your permission to send him.'

The commander said, 'Do not tell anyone that you have told me of this.' Then he sent the young man away.

The commander called two of his officers to approach him. 'Prepare two hundred soldiers with seventy horsemen and a further two hundred spearmen to go to Caesarea, at nine o'clock tonight,' he said. 'Have horses for Paul to ride so that he may be taken safely to Governor Felix,' he added. Then the commander wrote a letter to the governor that explained the situation with Paul. The commander, who was called Claudius Lysias, spoke of the murderous plot against Paul and his decision to send Paul to the governor at once.

The commander also told Governor Felix that he ordered Paul's accusers to present their case against Paul to the governor personally.

So, the soldiers followed orders, and took Paul to Caesarea. They delivered the letter to Governor Felix and handed Paul over to him. After reading the letter, the governor asked Paul where he was from. When he found out that Paul was from Cilicia, he said, 'I will hear your case when your accusers arrive.' And he commanded that Paul be keep under guard at Herod's palace.

WHAT'S THE POINT:

Paul's life was in danger … again! The plotters were so keen to kill Paul, that they planned to fast until they had succeeded. But Paul was still in Jerusalem. Paul trusted God to work out his plan to get him to Rome. God used Paul's nephew to help make it happen. By raising the alarm, the soldiers would step up to protect Paul until he would be able to stand before Caesar in Rome. Then Paul would testify to the truth about Jesus there, just as Jesus promised he would. Jesus is faithful to his promises. He uses ordinary people to further his plans and purposes for the world. We must trust Jesus, even if things look impossible to us.

LOOK BACK:

Read Psalm 3:1-8

King David wrote this Psalm. God's people have many enemies. But God is with his people. God protects his people. Therefore do not be afraid but ask God for help in times of trouble.

CHECK THIS OUT:

Read Luke 6:27-36

Jesus commands his followers to do what God has done, and to love our enemies.

THINK:

How does knowing God encourage you to trust him when things are difficult?

RISKY BUSINESS
Acts 24:1-27

When five days had passed, Ananias the high priest came down to Caesarea. Some elders and a lawyer called Tertullus came with him. They brought their charges against Paul before Governor Felix. When Paul came in to the trial, Tertullus began to speak.

'Most excellent Felix,' he said, 'we have enjoyed much peace since you became governor. We are grateful to you for bringing about many important reforms that are good for our country. I do not want to take up too much of your time, so I ask you to listen for just a few moments. This man is a bother. He incites rioting among the Jews all over the Roman Empire. He is the main leader of the Nazarene sect. He even tried to defile the temple, but we arrested him. Examine him yourself, and you will learn the truth about these charges that we bring against him.'

They confirmed the accusations were true. The Jews joined in the attack against Paul asserting that the accusations were true.

Governor Felix looked at Paul and nodded his head, meaning it was Paul's turn to speak.

'I know that you have ruled over the nation for many years, so I am happy to make my defence before you,' Paul began. 'It was no more than twelve days ago that I went to worship in Jerusalem. You can find that out yourself. These men did not find me arguing with anyone or provoking the people to riot, either in the temple, the synagogue, or anywhere else in the city. They cannot prove any of their charges against me. But

I will tell you this: I worship the God of our ancestors according to the Way, which they call a sect. I believe everything written in the Law and the Prophets. I have the same hope that these men have - that all people, whether good or bad, will rise from death. So, I always try to have a clear conscience before God and all people.

'Having been away for several years, I came to bring my people gifts for the poor and present offerings. As I was doing this, they found me in the temple. There was no crowd or uproar. But some Jews from Asia were there. They should be here before you, making accusations, if they have any to make against me. Or let these men tell you what offence I had committed when I stood before the council. The only thing that I shouted out when I was before them was this: "I am on trial because I believe in the resurrection from the dead."'

Felix knew about the Way, and he decided to halt proceedings. 'When the Roman commander, Claudius Lysias comes here, I will give you my decision,' he said. Felix ordered the officer to keep Paul under guard but give him some freedoms, such as allowing his friends to tend to any needs that he may have.

A number of days passed. Felix came with his Jewish wife Drusilla, to hear Paul speak about faith in Jesus Christ. Felix became unsettled when Paul spoke of the judgement to come, and sent him away, saying, 'I will hear you again, if I get the opportunity.' At the same time, he hoped for a bribe from Paul. Felix often sent for Paul and talked with him. He did this for two years. As a favour to the Jews, he kept Paul in prison that entire time. Then Felix was replaced as governor by a man called Porcius Festus.

WHAT'S THE POINT:

Paul is back in court in Caesarea. The false claims against Paul were a result of the Jews constant rejection of Paul's message about Jesus the Messiah. Felix held back his decision. He kept Paul in prison for two years until he was replaced as Governor. During those two years, Felix and his wife listened to Paul speak about faith in Jesus Christ. Sometimes we defend the gospel. Sometimes we take risks, telling people the truth about sin, Christ's rescue, and judgement.

CHECK IT OUT:

Read Mark 6:17-20

Governor Felix and King Herod were alike. Both of them loved to listen to their imprisoned preachers. But they both refused to repent of their sins and put their trust in Jesus as Saviour and Lord.

THINK:

What are the risks of telling an unbelieving friend or family member about Jesus?

IT'S A PRIVILEGE

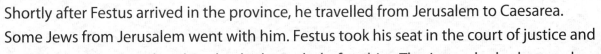

Acts 25:1-12

Shortly after Festus arrived in the province, he travelled from Jerusalem to Caesarea. Some Jews from Jerusalem went with him. Festus took his seat in the court of justice and ordered Paul to be brought before him. The Jews who had come down from Jerusalem laid charges against Paul, although they could not prove any of them. Then Paul answered in his defence. 'I have not done anything wrong against the law of the Jews, nor against the temple, not even against Caesar himself,' he said.

Festus wanted to do the Jews a favour, so he asked Paul, 'Are you willing to go up to Jerusalem and face trial before me there?'

'I am standing in the court of Caesar. This is where I should be tried,' replied Paul. 'I have done nothing wrong to the Jews, as you rightly know,' he continued. 'If I am a criminal deserving of the death penalty, then

so be it. But if none of their accusations are true, no one can hand me over to them. I make my appeal to Caesar.'

Festus consulted his council. Then he said to Paul, 'You have made an appeal to Caesar; therefore, you shall go to Caesar.'

WHAT'S THE POINT:

It feels like the same trial but with a new judge! The Jews attempted to get Paul moved back to Jerusalem. Then they could kill him on the way. Although Festus considered the move, Paul appealed to Caesar. As a Roman citizen on trial for his life, he had the right to be tried by the emperor. Paul was willing to die for his faith in Christ. However, he was not, willing to die for some false charges from the Jews. Going to Rome would give Paul more opportunities to preach the good news about Jesus. We should use whatever privilege we have to open up ways to talk about Jesus.

THINK:

Do you wonder what happened to those hungry and thirsty would-be assassins we met in Jerusalem? Two years is a long time to go without food and drink!

GOOD NEWS FOR KINGS

Acts 25:13 – 26:32

Some days later, King Agrippa and his sister Bernice came to Caesarea to meet Festus. After they had been there for many days, Festus told the king of Paul's situation.

'I would like to hear Paul myself,' said King Agrippa.

'I will have him brought before you tomorrow,' replied Festus.

The next day Paul was brought before King Agrippa and Bernice in the great hall. The room was full of the leading and important people of the city.

'King Agrippa, and all who are here today,' said Festus, 'this man has been accused of wrongdoing by the Jews. They have begged me to take his life. But I can find nothing to suggest that he deserves to die. He has appealed to Caesar, but I am finding it hard to write anything definite about him. Perhaps from this examination today, I may have something to write about him. It seems unreasonable to send a prisoner to Rome without saying what crimes he has been accused of.'

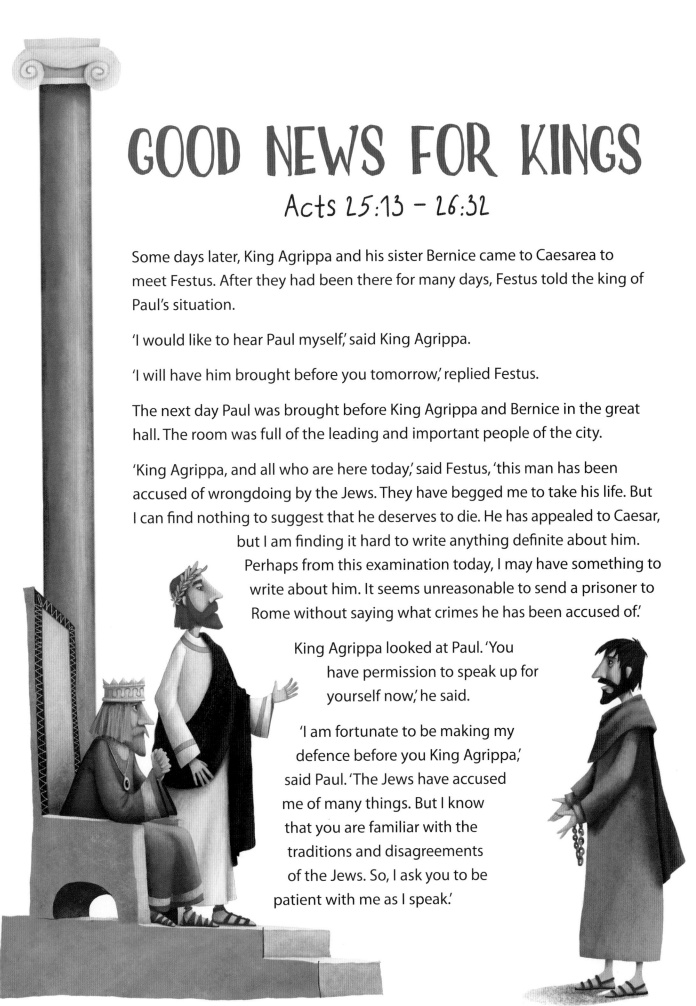

King Agrippa looked at Paul. 'You have permission to speak up for yourself now,' he said.

'I am fortunate to be making my defence before you King Agrippa,' said Paul. 'The Jews have accused me of many things. But I know that you are familiar with the traditions and disagreements of the Jews. So, I ask you to be patient with me as I speak.'

Then Paul began to carefully explain how he was converted from his strict life as a Pharisee, to become an apostle of the risen Christ. He spoke of the good news of forgiveness of sins through repentance and faith in Jesus.

As Paul was saying all these things, Festus shouted to him. 'Paul, you have gone mad! Your great learning has driven you around the bend!'

'I am not mad, most excellent Festus!' replied Paul. 'My words are true and reasonable,' he said. 'The king knows all about these things. That is why I am speaking boldly. Nothing has escaped the king's notice because it has all been done in the open and not in a dark corner somewhere.'

'King Agrippa, do you believe the prophets?' asked Paul. 'I know you do.'

The King looked at Paul and said, 'Do you think that you will make me a Christian in such a short period of time?'

Paul replied, 'Whether it is a short time or a long time, it is my prayer to God that you and everyone else who hears me today, might become what I am, except for the chains of course!'

Then King Agrippa and Governor Festus, along with Bernice and those who sat with them, got up and left the hall. They said to each other, 'This man is not doing anything that deserves death, or prison.'

King Agrippa turned to Festus and said, 'This man could have been freed if he had not appealed to Caesar.'

WHAT'S THE POINT:

Another trial, another chance to testify to the amazing grace of God. Paul himself received that grace on the Damascus Road. Paul testified to the authorities how God saved him, forgave him, and gave him a big family, through faith in Jesus. And the way was open for everyone, including his judges, to know God's grace for themselves too. Jesus is the only way that humanity can be put right with God. If only they would be like Paul and believe in Jesus!

CHECK IT OUT:

Read Matthew 10:28 and Proverbs 9:10

Do not fear people. The worst that they can do is nothing compared to what God can do!

THINK:

What should you do if you are afraid to tell your friends about Jesus because they might think you are mad?

A DANGEROUS JOURNEY
Acts 27:1-44

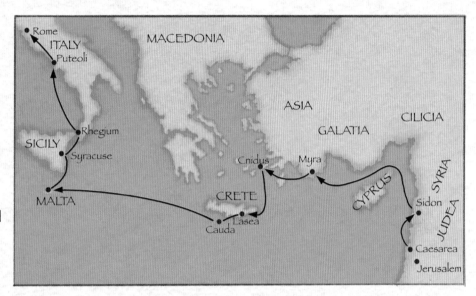

It was decided that Paul should sail to Italy. With a number of other prisoners, Paul was handed over to an army officer of the Augustan battalion. The officer was called Julius. They boarded the ship which was set to sail along the coast of Asia. The next day they arrived at Sidon. Julius was kind to Paul and gave him the freedom to visit his friends and refresh himself.

When they left there, they sailed along the coast of Cyprus, as the winds blew against them. They came to Myra, a city in the region of Lycia. Julius found a ship from Alexandria that was sailing to Italy, and he put his prisoners on it. For many days it was slow going. The winds were not favourable. Eventually they came to the place known as 'Fair Havens' near the city of Lasea. A lot of time had passed by. The journey onward was now dangerous because winter was approaching.

Paul warned them, 'Sirs, I can see that this voyage will be dangerous. There will be much damage to the cargo, to the ship, and even to our own lives.'

But Julius paid little attention to what Paul said. He listened to the captain and the owner of the ship instead. It was not a good harbour to stay in for the winter. Most of the men were in favour of setting sail for Phoenix in Crete, which was a good place to spend the winter.

They set off and sailed along the coast of Crete. But a wild wind blew off the land and took the ship further out to sea. Then they came near a small island called Cauda. The men tried to secure the ship with ropes. As they were blown further off course, they became afraid that they may be run aground on the sandbars of Syrtis. So, they dropped their sails and were set adrift.

The storm became ferocious. The men threw the ship's cargo and rigging overboard to lighten the load. But they could not see the sun or stars for days. As the storm raged on, the men gave up all hope of being saved.

They had gone without food for a long time when Paul stood up and said, 'Sirs, you should have listened to me and not sailed from Crete. You could have avoided all this damage and loss. But take courage. There will be no loss of life among you, only the ship. An angel of my God whom I worship, came to me tonight and said, "Do not be afraid, Paul. You must stand trial before Caesar. See how God answers your prayers. In his grace, he has given you the lives of all those who sail with you." So, take courage men, because I trust in God that it shall be exactly as he has told me. However, we must run aground on some island.'

It was the fourteenth night. The storm continued to toss the ship about the Mediterranean Sea. At midnight, some sailors felt they were getting close to land. They dropped a line into the water with a weight tied to it. The water was forty metres deep. A short while later they did it again and the reading was thirty metres. They were afraid that the ship would hit rocks, so they cast four anchors off the back of the boat. The sailors wanted to leave the ship, so they dropped the lifeboat into the water. But Paul said to Julius, 'Unless these men stay on the ship, you cannot be saved.' The soldiers on board cut the ropes of the lifeboat and watched it drift away.

At daybreak, Paul encouraged them all to eat some food. 'It will give you strength,' he said. 'Not a hair on your heads will perish.' Then he took some bread and thanked God for it. He broke it and ate. There were 276 people on board. Everyone ate and was encouraged. And when they had eaten enough, they threw the remaining cargo of wheat overboard to make the ship lighter.

Later that day, they saw land that was not known to them. They saw a bay with a sandy beach. They thought they could run the ship ashore on it. They cut the anchors loose and left them in the sea. They untied the ropes that were attached to the steering paddles, and they hoisted the sail. The ship moved towards the shore but all of a sudden, it hit some rocks under the water. The front of the ship was stuck while the strong surf pounded the back of the ship, breaking it to pieces. The soldiers decided to kill the prisoners rather than allowing any of them to swim away and escape. But Julius wanted to protect Paul, so he stopped them from carrying out their plan. He ordered that anyone who could swim should jump overboard and head for the land. The others could float ashore, using planks or bits of the ship. This is how everyone reached the shore safely.

WHAT'S THE POINT:

The journey was dangerous. At times the men thought they would all die. But God promised to get Paul to Rome, and he was not going to break his promise. The men had skill and intelligence to work together through the storm. At times they were very afraid. Paul encouraged them to trust God, eat something and keep their strength up. God would keep them safe. And he did. They got to shore in one piece. Neither people nor creation can stop God from keeping his promises.

LOOK BACK:

Read Acts 2:23

God is sovereign (in complete charge) and we are responsible for our actions.

THINK:

Nothing and no one can stop God from keeping his promises.

HE'S A GOD! NO I'M NOT!

Acts 28:1-16

The survivors arrived safely ashore on the island of Malta. They were kindly treated by the locals. It was cold and started to rain, so the islanders lit a fire for the men and welcomed all of them. Paul gathered a bundle of sticks and threw them onto the fire. A snake was driven out by the heat and bit Paul, attaching itself to his hand. The islanders saw the snake dangling from his hand.

'This man is a murderer, no doubt about it,' they said to each other. 'He may have escaped from the dangers of the sea, but it seems like the goddess Justice will not allow him to live,' they said.

Meanwhile, Paul simply shook the snake off his hand and into the fire. The islanders watched him closely. They were waiting for the poison from the snake to take effect. Perhaps it would make him swell up, or even just fall down dead. They waited, and they waited. But nothing happened! Paul suffered no harm from the snakebite. When the islanders saw that Paul was okay, they changed their minds about him. He wasn't a murderer; he was a god!

In the area were lands that belonged to the chief of the island. His name was Publius. He also welcomed the men warmly and he looked after them very well for a few days. His father was terribly ill in bed with fever. Paul went in to him and prayed. He placed his hands on the sick man and he was immediately healed. After this happened, many other islanders who were ill with sickness and disease came to Paul and were healed too.

The men were greatly honoured by the islanders. When it was time to set sail, they put whatever they needed on the ship.

When three months had passed, they left on a ship from Alexandria. At the front of the ship was a large wooden sculpture of the Greek gods called **Castor** and **Pollux**. The ship had spent the winter at the island. They sailed to Syracuse, then to Rhegium and Puteoli, before finally arriving at Rome. When the disciples of Jesus in Rome heard of Paul's arrival, they came to meet him, from as far away as the towns of the Forum of Appius and Three Taverns. When Paul saw them, he gave thanks to God and was greatly encouraged. When they came to the city of Rome, the prisoners were handed over to the captain of the guard. But Paul was allowed to live on his own with a soldier guarding him all the time.

WHAT'S THE POINT:

The islanders were pleasant, kind, and generous people. But they were superstitious sinners in need of a Saviour. The viper attack on Paul shows this to be true. They believed that if someone suffered greatly, they must have sinned greatly too. When Paul suffered no harm, they then thought he was a god. But Paul kept telling them the gospel. The miracles of healing were signs confirming that the gospel that Paul was speaking to them was the truth. Then it was on to Rome, the final stop of his remarkable journey. Paul's example to us is that we should always be willing to bear witness to Jesus, wherever we may be.

CHECK THIS OUT:

Read Acts 14:23 and 2 Corinthians 12:12

God confirmed that the message of his grace was true by enabling his apostles to do miracles.

THINK:

Paul was encouraged by the Christians in Rome who kept him company on his final march into the city. Does the company of your Christian friends encourage you? Do you encourage them with your company, especially in hard times?

IT IS ALL ABOUT JESUS
Acts 28:17-31

After three days, Paul called the local Jewish leaders together for a meeting. He said to them, 'Fellow Israelites, even though I did nothing wrong against our people or the traditions that have been handed down to us from our ancestors, still I was made a prisoner in Jerusalem and handed over to the Romans. After questioning me, the Romans wanted to set me free. They could find no good reason for giving me the death penalty. But the Jews protested, and I was forced to make my appeal to Caesar. I did not want to make any charge against my own people. This is why I have asked to see and speak with you all. I am chained up because of the hope that Israel has in the Messiah.'

'We have not received any letters from Judea about you,' they replied. 'No one from there coming to Rome has reported or said anything bad about you. We would like to hear what you think, because everyone speaks against this group that you belong to.'

They arranged a day to come to the place where Paul was staying. A large number of them came to hear him speak. From morning till night Paul taught them about the kingdom of God. He wanted to persuade them from the Law of Moses and the Prophets that Jesus is the Messiah. Some of them believed but others did not. The group was divided.

Paul said, 'The Holy Spirit said through the prophet Isaiah,

"Go and tell this people, You will listen, you will not understand.

You will look with your eyes, but you will not see,

because the people's heart has grown hard.

They can hardly hear with their ears

and they have closed their eyes.

Otherwise, they would see with their eyes,

hear with their ears

and understand with their hearts and turn back to me and I shall heal them.'"

Then Paul said, 'Know then, all of you, that God's gospel of salvation has been sent to the Gentiles. They will listen!'

The group then left him.

Paul lived in his rented house for two years. He warmly welcomed anyone who came to see him. And no one stopped Paul telling people about the kingdom of God and boldly teaching them about the Lord Jesus Christ.

WHAT'S THE POINT:

While some Jews believed the good news about Jesus, others did not. Many Gentiles believed in Jesus, but others did not. It is sad when people do not listen to the good news about Jesus and believe in him. But the gospel will keep spreading throughout God's world. God uses his children to bring the good news of Jesus to others. And you are part of God's plan in doing that. Remember, it is all about Jesus!

LOOK BACK:

Read Isaiah 6:9-10 and Matthew 13:14-15

The Jews had eyes to see, ears to hear, but hard hearts that failed to respond in the right way to Jesus the Messiah. They did not believe in him as Saviour nor submit to him as Lord.

CHECK THIS OUT:

Read Acts 1:8

Jesus' words are fulfilled in the book of Acts. Can you think how?

THINK:

Throughout Acts, Jesus keeps his promises. Does that deepen your trust in him? Will that help you live your Christian life more faithfully than you do at present? Do you believe in Christ for yourself or has your heart been hardened in unbelief?

WHAT DOES IT MEAN?

Areopagus – this is not a building; it is a group of people.

Apostle – an apostle was a man chosen by Jesus to follow him throughout the course of his ministry on earth.

Brethren – brothers; used when referring to members of a group.

Castor and **Pollux** were Greek deities responsible for smooth sailing.

Circumcise – to cut off the foreskin of a penis. This happened to boys who were eight days old as a physical sign of belonging to the nation of Israel.

Church – a new family of people, those who are forgiven by Jesus, and who serve Jesus as King, love each other, and tell other people about God.

Chance – something that is not planned.

Covenant – a covenant is like a contract full of promises that is binding on both parties.

Disciple – someone who follows Jesus. The word 'disciple' means student, or learner.

Epicureans - the Epicureans believed that the world is ruled by *chance*.

Grace – a gift of love, mercy and forgiveness offered to someone who does not deserve it.

Flogged – beaten hard, usually with whips, or rods.

Garrison – an army barracks or fort.

Hellenists – Gentiles who spoke the Greek language.

Hypocrite – someone who pretends to be virtuous but isn't.

Idol – an idol is something (or someone) that is worshipped instead of the true and living God.

Imperishable – something that can never rot and die but lasts forever.

Inheritance – something that a person receives because he or she is a family member and heir.

Messiah – a Hebrew word meaning 'Anointed One' of God. The Greek word for 'Anointed One' is 'Christ'.

Pentecost – a Jewish harvest celebration that happened 50 days after the Feast of Passover.

Persecute – to harass, hurt, or kill someone for his or her love for Jesus Christ.

Prophet – a special messenger of God in the Old Testament.

Sabbath – God created the world in six days, and he rested on the seventh day. The Sabbath (the seventh day of the week) was given by God to his people so that they could rest from working and focus on worshipping him.

Signs – a word which is often used in Acts to describe the miracles which point us to Jesus and heaven.

Silver piece – a silver coin that is worth about a day's wage.

Stoics – the Stoics believed that there is nothing beyond the grave.

Synagogue – a building where Jews meet for worship.

Tanner – a person who tans animal hides and turns them into leather.

Transgressions – things that are wrong and displease God.

Way – this is an abbreviated term to refer to Christianity which is the 'way of salvation' (Acts 16:17) or 'the way of the Lord' (Acts 18:25).

CHRISTIAN FOCUS PUBLICATIONS

Christian Focus Publications publishes books for adults and children under its four main imprints: Christian Focus, CF4K, Mentor and Christian Heritage. Our books reflect our conviction that God's Word is reliable and Jesus is the way to know him, and live for ever with him.

Our children's publication list covers pre-school to early teens. We also publish personal and family devotional titles, biographies and inspirational stories that children will love.

From pre-school board books to teenage apologetics, we have it covered!

Christian Focus Publications Ltd, Geanies House, Fearn, Ross-shire, IV20 1TW, Scotland, United Kingdom.

www.christianfocus.com

CHRISTIAN FOCUS PUBLICATIONS

Christian Focus | Christian Heritage | CF4K | Mentor